fusible magic

EASY MIX & MATCH SHAPES—THOUSANDS OF DESIGN POSSIBILITIES

Includes 100 Blocks, 9 Quilt Projects

NANCY JOHNSON-SREBRO

C&T PUBLISHING

Text copyright © 2010 by Silver Star, Inc.

Artwork copyright © 2010 by C&T Publishing, Inc.

Publisher: Amy Marson

Creative Director: Gailen Runge

Acquisitions Editor: Susanne Woods

Editor: Liz Aneloski

Technical Editor: Ellen Pahl

Copyeditor/Proofreader: Wordfirm Inc.

Cover/Book Designer: Kristen Yenche

Production Coordinator: Zinnia Heinzmann

Production Editor: Alice Mace Nakanishi

Illustrator: Tim Manibusan

Photography by Christina Carty-Francis and Diane Pedersen of C&T Publishing, Inc., unless otherwise noted

Published by C&T Publishing, Inc., P.O. Box 1456, Lafayette, CA 94549

Library of Congress Cataloging-in-Publication Data

Johnson-Srebro, Nancy.

 Fusible magic : easy mix & match shapes : thousands of design possibilities includes 100 blocks, 9 quilt projects / Nancy Johnson-Srebro.

    p. cm.

 ISBN 978-1-57120-858-3

 1. Quilting--Patterns. 2. Patchwork--Patterns. I. Title.

 TT835.J5866 2010

 746.46'041--dc22

                                2009034657

Printed in China

10 9 8 7 6 5 4 3 2 1

Dedication

This book is dedicated to volunteers who work tirelessly to make life better for others. I applaud you for your hard work.

Acknowledgments

Thank you to my quilt team: Liz Aneloski, Karen Bolesta, Carol Brown, Karen Brown, Debbie Donowski, Allison Dowling, Robin Fleming, Nancy Jones, Beth Anne Lowrie, Janet McCarroll, Vicki Novajosky, Ellen Pahl, Pam Quentin, Laura Reidenbach, Rocky Sidorek, and Casey and Jenny Srebro. We had fun, didn't we?!

Special thanks to Janet McCarroll for her superb machine quilting talents.

As always, I'd like to extend a big thank-you to the entire C&T staff and my longtime editors and friends, Liz Aneloski and Ellen Pahl.

contents

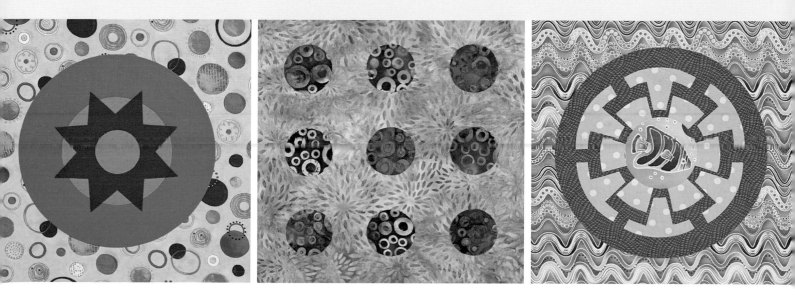

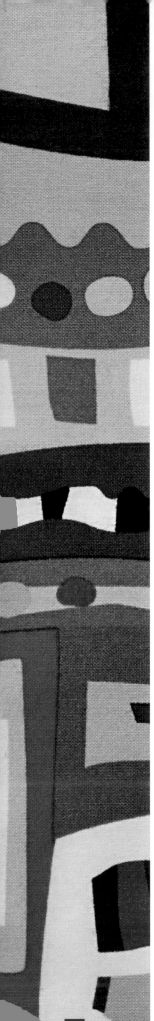

introduction

It's funny how life can take unexpected twists and turns. Honestly, I didn't think I'd be writing another book after *Big One-Star Quilts by Magic*. My husband and I lost three parents in a three-year period, and I was drained from the emotional loss. The joy of quilting had waned, so I took a year off from writing, designing, and doing any serious quiltmaking. I needed a change of pace and decided to work full time on something near and dear to my heart: making quilts for ill children. That year, I cut, sewed, and pressed my way through more than 300 quilts for our local organization, Project Donating Joy.

One day I experimented, fusing some circles onto a few of the pieced baby quilts. I quickly became addicted to fusing circles, and then I made some prototypes using other shapes. It went on and on … and, as they say, the rest is history.

I shared these new designs with my quilt teams and brought my template ideas to C&T Publishing and Prym Consumer. Both companies loved the concept and templates … so off I went to write another book!

I've designed and included 100 fusible block patterns in this book. Yes, that's right—my favorite 100 fusible blocks! Most of these blocks take only 30 minutes or less to make. All the appliqué patterns are included, so you can make your own templates, but, perhaps easier, you can also buy the ready-made templates at your local quilt or craft store. They're called Flip-N-Cut Magic Templates by Omnigrid and are made by Prym Consumer. I think you'll love them.

I'm also sharing nine quick and fun projects that require minimal sewing (one actually requires no sewing at all). Best of all, these ideas have come from the heartache of loss and the joy of helping hospitalized children. You just never know about life.

—Nancy

no-fail fusing basics

I used Steam-A-Seam 2 for all the projects in this book, so my hints and tips are based on this brand of fusible web.

supplies

- **Fusible web**   There are many brands and types of fusible web on the market. Find the one that works best for you and follow the manufacturer's instructions.

- **Template material**   Use clear, stiff plastic to trace and cut out the template patterns.

- **Fine-point permanent marker**   You'll use the fine-point marker for tracing and labeling the templates.

- **Mechanical pencil**   I prefer mechanical pencils for drawing around the templates on the paper backing of the fusible web.

- **4½″ and 6½″ Omnigrid scissors**   The scissors you use must be sharp right to the point of the blade—otherwise you'll have trouble getting clean-looking edges on the appliqué shapes.

- **Appliqué pressing cloth**   This 11″ × 17″ cloth is nonstick and heat resistant. Place it over your appliqué pieces before pressing. It will help keep the bottom of your iron from accidentally picking up any glue from the fusible web.

- **28mm and 45mm rotary cutters**   You will use these cutters for cutting fusible shapes in halves and quarters, and cutting out background and border fabrics. If you purchase Flip-N-Cut Magic Templates by Omnigrid, the smaller 28mm rotary cutter can be used to cut around the circle templates.

- **Revolving cutting mat** (*optional*)   This type of mat is very helpful when cutting around the circle templates.

making templates

If you will be using the shapes on pages 56–62 many times, you'll find it helpful to make sturdy templates. Place a sheet of clear plastic template material over the desired shape and trace it with a permanent marker. Cut out the shape and label it with the permanent marker. It's that simple!

choosing fabrics

I have found that tightly woven fabrics work best for the appliqué shapes. If the fabrics are not tightly woven, the edges of the appliqué pieces will fray easily. Batik fabrics work especially well.

fusing with steam-a-seam 2

For some helpful hints and important tips, I suggest that you read the Top No-Fail Tips (page 9) before you begin.

Step One

Cut a piece of paper-lined fusible web larger than the shape you'll be tracing. There is a paper liner on both sides of Steam-A-Seam 2. One of the liners adheres to the web more than the other. To determine which liner is more heavily stuck to the web, bend back one of the corners and check. That's the liner you'll want to trace the design on.

Place the template on top of the paper liner that is more heavily adhered to the web and trace around it.

Step Two

Press the fabric, wrong side up, just before you're ready to use it. Quickly remove and discard the bottom paper liner without the tracing. While the fabric is still warm, position the web, adhesive side down, on the wrong side of the fabric. The heat from pressing the fabric will be just enough to secure the piece of web and the paper liner. The paper liner with the drawn shape will be on top of the web and facing you.

Step Three

Cut out the shape on the drawn line. You'll be cutting through three layers—paper liner, web, and fabric.

Step Four

Peel off the remaining paper liner (not the web) and position the cut-out shape on the right side of the block or background fabric.

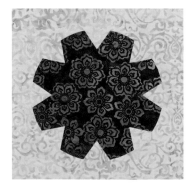

Step Five

Place an appliqué pressing cloth over the design and press it using steam for 10–15 seconds for cotton fabrics. I remove the pressing cloth and press again on the front for 5–10 seconds. I then check the edges of the appliqué piece to see if it's securely fused to the background fabric. If not, I turn the block over and press from the wrong side for 5 seconds. A common mistake is to not press long enough—the edges of the appliqué piece will not bond well and will loosen over time.

cutting shapes into halves and quarters

Cutting the appliqué shapes into halves or quarters will give you endless possibilities with the template shapes, and it's easy to do. Cut out the appliqué piece (with the paper liner still attached), then cut the shape into halves or quarters using a ruler and rotary cutter. Remove the liner and fuse the pieces to the block or background.

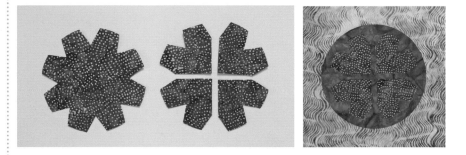

bonus cutouts

You can also get bonus cutouts, and this is really exciting! These clever shapes gave an unexpected artistic flair to some of the blocks. To get these extra cutouts, simply draw a circle of the same size diameter as the desired flower, star, or other shape. Next, draw the desired shape in the center of the circle. After adhering the circle to the fabric, cut out the circle and then the bonus sections. Remove the liner and fuse the pieces to the block or background.

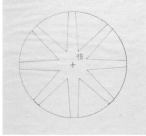

top no-fail tips

■ Be sure to press all wrinkles from the fabric before applying the fusible web and cutting the shapes. The wrinkles won't press out later! The same is true of the background fabric you're fusing to.

■ I always cut my background pieces at least ½" larger and trim to the unfinished size after fusing. Sometimes the background piece becomes slightly stretched while you are using steam to fuse the appliqué pieces in place. You can always trim, but you can't add on!

■ When cutting the desired shape, move the hand holding the appliqué piece, not the hand holding the scissors. This method will ensure that the shapes have nice edges.

■ If you will be fusing multiple layers of appliqué, you might want to use a lighter-weight web such as Lite Steam-A-Seam 2 for the second, third, or successive layers. Layering regular-weight web will make the pieces feel stiff.

■ Fold the background square in half in both directions to find its center and use these center crease lines to help position the appliqué pieces.

■ If your quilt will be used and washed a lot, you might want to finish the edges of the appliqué pieces with stitching. This will guarantee that the fused edges won't come loose. Use one of the many decorative stitches on your sewing machine to do this.

■ Cutting a shape out of a circle can be difficult if you start the cut with scissors. Instead, use a 1" × 6" ruler and a rotary cutter to make a small cut on the drawn template shape; then continue with scissors. This method helps prevent fraying of the fabric edges when you are starting the cut.

■ To prevent hand fatigue while cutting out the appliqué pieces, use scissors that are the correct size for you.

■ Keep a sharp blade in your rotary cutter if you're cutting around the purchased acrylic circle templates. A dull blade leaves frayed edges.

■ Glue from fusible web can build up on rotary cutter and scissor blades. You'll know this is happening if the edges of the appliqué pieces begin to look rough. Clean the blades with rubbing alcohol or nail polish remover, then wipe dry. Be very careful when using either solvent around your fabrics and equipment.

■ A revolving cutting mat makes rotary cutting circles very easy because you're able to keep one hand on the template while spinning the mat with your other hand.

■ If you're using the shapes for scrapbooking, remember to draw the shapes on the back of the paper, not the front.

■ I found it easy to misplace the templates. To avoid this, store the templates in a clear plastic zip bag or clear container. See page 45 for an innovative solution from Beth Anne Lowrie.

Happy Go Lucky by Pam Quentin, quilted by Janet McCarroll, 36" × 40"

Just like a bouquet of wildflowers, this wallhanging goes together quickly, with simply sensational results. Circles in the border add lightness and highlight the floral bouquet.

yardage and cutting

Place fusible web on the wrong side of the fabric pieces indicated with a ★ before cutting the shapes, following the manufacturer's directions.

⅞ yard light for background

Cut 1 rectangle 24½" × 28½" for center block.

★ Cut twelve 4" circles for border (template page 61).

1⅛ yards blue for borders and binding

Cut 2 strips 6¼" × 28½" for side borders.

Cut 2 strips 6¼" × 36" for top and bottom borders.

8" × 12" rectangle tan for vase

★ Cut 1 rectangle 3" × 4½".

★ Cut one 7" circle (template page 61)

Various scraps for circles and flowers (circle templates page 61, flower templates pages 56–60)

★ Cut one 1" circle, three 2" circles, one 3" circle, one 4" circle, and one 7" circle.

★ Cut 2 using 6A.

★ Cut 1 using 6B.

★ Cut 1 using 7A.

★ Cut 1 using 7B.

★ Cut 1 using 8B.

★ Cut 2 using 9B.

Various scraps for stems and leaves

★ Cut 2 rectangles ⅝" × 11" and 1 rectangle ⅝" × 7" for straight stems.

★ Cut 2 curved stems (template page 62).

★ Cut 1 of each leaf (templates page 58).

1⅝ yards fusible web (based on 10" width)

1⅜ yards for backing

assembling the quilt top

Step One

To make the vase, cut 2½" from the bottom of the tan 7" circle. Use this piece for the top of the vase, the 3" × 4½" rectangle for the middle of the vase, and the remainder of the circle for the bottom.

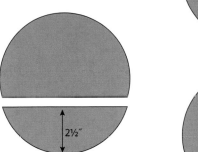
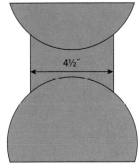

Step Two

Referring to the diagram, arrange the appliqué pieces and fuse them to the background. Note that both the 9B and 8B shapes were slightly altered to give them even more pizzazz.

Sew the borders to the center block. Fuse the circles to the border.

rainbow sherbet

Rainbow Sherbet by Liz Aneloski, 27½″ × 27½″

Choose yummy colors to make the appliqués float and turn. This design uses the inside and outside parts of only one template shape. Use button embellishments to add texture and sparkle. Super easy!

yardage and cutting

Place fusible web on the wrong side of the fabric pieces indicated with a ★ before cutting the shapes, following the manufacturer's directions.

If you choose a white print for the appliqués, be sure the background fabrics are light enough and the white fabric is opaque enough, so that the background print doesn't show through the white fabric.

⅜ yard each yellow and pink for background blocks

Cut 8 squares 5″ × 5″ of each fabric.

⅜ yard each yellow and pink for borders

Cut 2 strips 5″ × 23″ of each fabric.

⅜ yard white-on-white print for appliqués

★ Cut six 6″ circles (template page 61).

⅝ yard fusible web (based on 18″ width)

1 yard for backing

⅜ yard for binding

Buttons*

58 ¼″ buttons, five ½″ buttons, ten 1″ buttons

Seed beads (optional)

Liz used Stitchin' Buttons by Dill Buttons

assembling the quilt top

Step One

Cut 6A (template page 56) from the center of each 6″ circle. See the tip on page 9 for the best way to begin cutting a shape out of the center of a circle.

Referring to the diagrams, cut and/or remove the sections from the outer circles and 6A as shown. The 6A pieces will be fused to the border, and the outer circles will be fused to the center. Leave 1 outer circle whole for the center of the wallhanging.

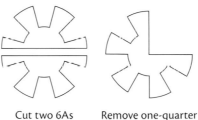

Cut two 6As in half.   Remove one-quarter from 4 of the 6A pieces.

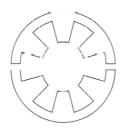

Cut 1 outer circle in half.

Remove one-quarter from 2 of the outer circles.

Remove one-quarter from 2 of the outer circles.

Step Two

Sew the background squares into 4 rows of 4 blocks each, alternating the prints. Sew the rows together.

Step Three

Add the borders using the partial seam method.

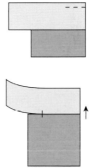

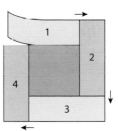

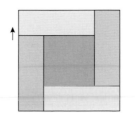

Step Four

Fuse the appliqués in place, referring to the quilt photo. Add button embellishments and seed beads if desired after quilting.

floral salute

Floral Salute by Pam Quentin, quilted by Janet McCarroll, 48" × 35"

Solitary blooms in stunning vases add an instant decorator touch to any room. Make four individual wallhangings or use them all together. Arrange these flowers no matter what the season and enjoy them all year round.

yardage and cutting

Place fusible web on the wrong side of the fabric pieces indicated with a ★ before cutting the shapes, following the manufacturer's directions.

⅞ yard light for background

Cut 1 rectangle 25½″ × 36½″ for center block.

1⅜ yards print for side and top borders and binding

Cut 2 strips 6¼″ × 29¼″ for side borders.

Cut 2 strips 6¼″ × 24¼″ for top border.

¼ yard print for bottom border

Cut 1 strip 4¼″ × 36½″.

Various scraps for vases

★ Cut 1 rectangle 3″ × 8″ of two different fabrics for skinny vases.

★ Cut 1 rectangle 6″ × 8″ of two different fabrics for wider vases.

Various scraps for circles and flowers

(circle templates on page 61, flower templates on pages 56–60)

★ Cut two 1″ circles, four 2″ circles, three 3″ circles, and three 4″ circles.

★ Cut 1 using 5A.

★ Cut 1 using 5B.

★ Cut 1 using 7A.

★ Cut 2 using 8B.

★ Cut 1 using 9A.

★ Cut 2 using 9B.

Various scraps of green for stems and leaves

★ Cut 1 rectangle ½″ × 14″ and 1 rectangle ½″ × 4″ for narrow stems.

★ Cut 2 rectangles 1″ × 9″ for wider stems.

★ Cut 1 rectangle ¾″ × 7″ for tall leaf.

★ Cut 1 curved stem and 2 leaves (template pages 59 and 62).

1½ yards fusible web (based on 18″ width)

1½ yards for backing

assembling the quilt top

Step One

To make the 2 wide vases, measure in 1½″ from the bottom corners of the 6″ × 8″ rectangles and mark with a pencil. Cut from the top right corner to the pencil mark on the right bottom of the rectangle. Do the same for the left side of each. To make the skinny, pointed leaf, trim 2 sides of the ¾″ × 7″ rectangle to form a narrow point.

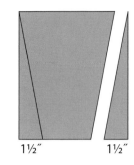

1½″   1½″

Step Two

Refer to the diagram to arrange the appliqués and fuse them to the background.

Sew the bottom border first and then add the side borders. Sew the 2 strips (6¼″ × 24¼″) for the top border together to make 1 long strip and add it to the top.

Debut designed by Jay McCarroll, sewn and quilted by Janet McCarroll, 30½″ × 30½″

This wallhanging is definitely a first! It is the first quilt made from Jay McCarroll's first line of fabric for FreeSpirit Fabrics. The print fabrics are from Jay's fabric line called Garden Friends and Woodland Wonderland. And, by the way, Jay is the first winner of the popular reality show *Project Runway!*

yardage and cutting

36 assorted print scraps for A

Cut 1 square 3½" × 3½" of each fabric.

9 assorted solid scraps for B

Cut 1 square 8½" × 8½" of each fabric.

9 assorted solid scraps for C

Cut 1 square 10½" × 10½" of each fabric.

2⅓ yards fusible web (based on 18" width)

Cut 9 squares 6½" × 6½" for A.

Cut 9 squares 8½" × 8½" for B.

1 yard for backing

½ yard for binding

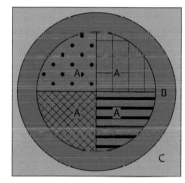

assembling the quilt top

Step One

Make 9 Four Patch blocks.

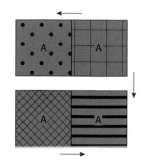

Place the 6½" squares of fusible web on the wrong sides of the Four Patch blocks. Cut a 6" circle from each Four Patch block (template page 61).

Step Two

Center a Four Patch circle on each B square and fuse.

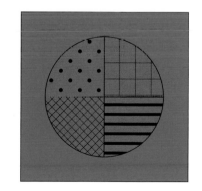

Place the 8½" squares of fusible web on the wrong sides of the B squares. Cut an 8" circle from each B square (template page 61).

Step Three

Fuse the 8" circles to the C squares. Sew a decorative stitch around the circles if desired.

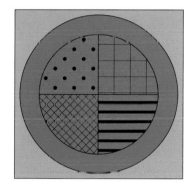

Make 9.

Step Four

Arrange the blocks. Sew the blocks into rows. Sew the rows together.

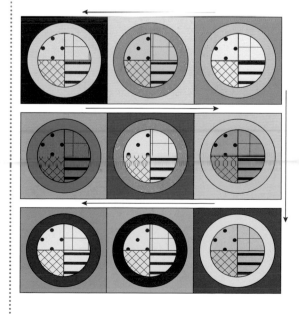

Rising Star Medallion by Nancy Johnson-Srebro, quilted by Janet McCarroll, 30½″ × 30½″

Make this elegant wallhanging to bring light into any room of your house. It is beautifully made in batiks and reminds me of light streaming through a stained-glass window in a cathedral.

yardage and cutting

Place fusible web on the wrong side of the fabric pieces indicated with a ★ before cutting the shapes, following the manufacturer's directions.

1¼ yards light for background

Cut 12 squares 8″ × 8″ for outer blocks.

Cut 1 square 15½″ × 15½″ for center block.

⅝ yard dark gold for binding and outside-edge triangles

Cut 28 squares 2½″ × 2½″.

¼ yard medium pink for center star

★ Cut 8 rectangles 2½″ × 6″.

½ yard dark pink for flower surrounding star points, small center flower, and outer stars

★ Cut 2 using 9A; cut into quarters to make 8 heart shapes (template page 60).

★ Cut 4 using 7A (template page 56).

★ Cut 1 using 7B (template page 60).

¼ yard light pink for center flower and circles for outer blocks

★ Cut 1 using 9A (template page 60).

★ Cut eight 1″ circles (template page 61).

⅛ yard green for circles in center and corner blocks

★ Cut five 3″ circles (template page 61).

1 square 3″ × 3″ light pink print for center circle

★ Cut one 2″ circle (template page 61).

¼ yard pink polka dot for flowers behind stars in outer blocks

★ Cut 4 using 7B (template page 60).

8 squares 5″ × 5″ assorted pink scraps for flowers in outer blocks

★ Cut 1 using 5B of each fabric (template page 57).

1¾ yards fusible web (based on 18″ width)

1 yard for backing

assembling the quilt top

Step One

Cut the corners off the 2½″ × 6″ pink rectangles at a 45° angle to form the diamond shapes.

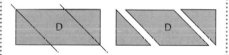

Position the diamonds to form a star, centered on the 15½″ square block. Place the 9A quarters so the edges are slightly underneath the diamond points.

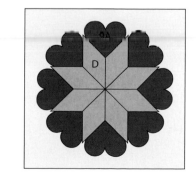

Center the remaining pieces in this order: 9A, 7B, 3″ circle, and 2″ circle. Fuse.

Step Two

Draw a pencil line diagonally from corner to corner on the wrong side of each gold 2½″ square. Position the squares on the corners of the 8½″ outer blocks. Stitch on the drawn lines. Trim the seam allowances ¼″ from the stitching lines. Fuse the appliqué pieces to the blocks.

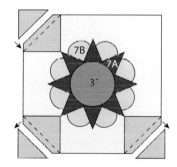

Corner blocks; make 4.

Top, bottom, and side blocks; make 8.

Step Three

Arrange the blocks and sew them into rows. Sew the rows together.

tropical nine patch

Tropical Nine Patch by Nancy Johnson-Srebro, quilted by Janet McCarroll, 36½" × 36½"

Nine simple blocks are all you need to create for this super quilt. Choose colors that are opposite each other on the color wheel for a dynamic, graphic effect.

yardage and cutting

Place fusible web on the wrong side of the fabric pieces indicated with a ★ before cutting the shapes, following the manufacturer's directions.

9 fat quarters orange for background and circles

Cut 9 squares 12½″ × 12½″.

★ Cut one 3″ circle from 4 of the fabrics (template page 61).

½ yard beige for circles and flowers

★ Cut five 8″ circles (template page 61).

Cut 8A (template page 58) from the centers of the 8″ circles. You will use 4 of the 8A pieces. See the tip on page 9 for cutting a shape out of the center of a circle.

¼ yard teal for circles and flowers

★ Cut 5 using 6B (template page 57).

★ Cut four 4″ circles (template page 61).

1¼ yards fusible web (based on 18″ width)

1¼ yards for backing

½ yard for binding

assembling the quilt top

Position the appliqué pieces and fuse them to the background squares. Arrange the blocks and sew them into rows. Sew the rows together.

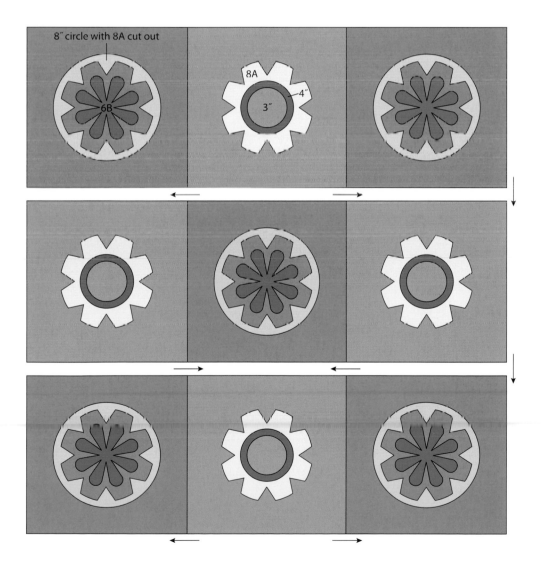

gathering basket

Gathering Basket by Nancy Johnson-Srebro, quilted by Janet McCarroll, 23″ × 23″

Batiks, flowers, quilts, and baskets—doesn't everyone love these?
What more could a quilter want!

yardage and cutting

Place fusible web on the wrong side of the fabric pieces indicated with a ★ before cutting the shapes, following the manufacturer's directions.

1 fat quarter yellow for background

Cut 1 square 17″ × 17″.

12″ × 12″ square purple for basket

★ Cut 1 rectangle 5″ × 10½″ for bottom.

★ Cut 1 rectangle 2½″ × 6½″ for handle.

9″ × 9″ square coral for cornerstones

Cut 4 squares 3½″ × 3½″.

⅓ yard teal for borders

Cut 4 strips 3½″ × 17″.

⅜ yard for binding

Assorted scraps for flowers, circles, and leaves (flower templates on pages 56–59, circle templates on page 61, leaf template on page 57)

★ Cut seven 1″ circles and three 2″ circles.

★ Cut 1 using 3A.

★ Cut 2 using 3B.

★ Cut 2 using 4A (including 4 bonus cutouts).

★ Cut 1 using 4B (including 6 bonus cutouts).

★ Cut 1 using 5A.

★ Cut 3 using 5B.

★ Cut 8 leaves.

1 yard fusible web (based on 18″ width)

⅞ yard for backing

assembling the quilt top

Arrange the pieces and fuse them to the background. Add the borders.

double the fun

Double the Fun by Nancy Johnson-Srebro, quilted by Janet McCarroll, 48½″ × 36½″

Have fun choosing two complementary fabrics and you'll have this crib-size quilt made in practically no time at all. I made this quilt top in two hours!

yardage and cutting

1⅓ yards light yellow for blocks

Cut 12 rectangles 6½″ × 12½″ (A).

Cut 12 rectangles 4½″ × 8½″ (B).

1⅓ yards dark blue for blocks

Cut 12 rectangles 6½″ × 12½″ (C).

Cut 12 rectangles 4½″ × 8½″ (D).

1⅔ yards fusible web (based on 18″ width)

Cut 12 squares 8½″ × 8½″ for B/D circle.

1½ yards for backing

½ yard for binding

assembling the quilt top

Step One

Sew an A rectangle and a C rectangle together. Make 12.

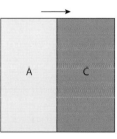

Step Two

Sew a B rectangle and a D rectangle together. Make 12.

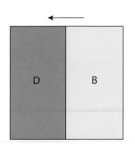

Place fusible web on the wrong side of each B/D block. Cut an 8″ circle from each B/D block (template page 61).

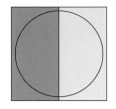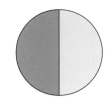

Step Three

Center the B/D circle on the A/C background square, making sure to align the seam allowances. Fuse.

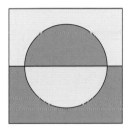

Make 12.

Step Four

Arrange the blocks. Sew the blocks into rows. Sew the rows together.

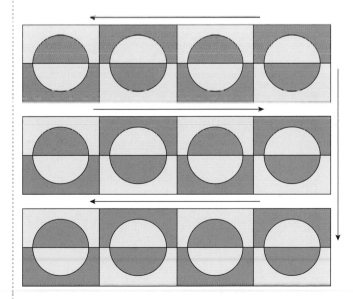

stars and stripes for all

Stars and Stripes for All by Nancy Johnson-Srebro, quilted by Janet McCarroll, 48½″ × 40″

H ere's a no-sew quilt that is perfect for beginners or just plain fun for anyone! Choose a red background, a white for stars and stripes, and a jaunty blue, and you're all set. This is a lap quilt, but you could make it smaller for a terrific patriotic banner.

yardage and cutting

Place fusible web on the wrong side of the fabric pieces indicated with a ★ before cutting the shapes, following the manufacturer's directions.

1⅞ yards red for background

Cut 1 rectangle 48½" × 40".

★ Cut five 8" circles (template page 61).

⅞ yard blue for squares

★ Cut 1 square 18" × 18" for center block.

★ Cut 4 squares 9½" × 9½" for corners.

⅞ yard white for stars and stripes

★ Cut 8 strips 2" × 15¾".

★ Cut 4 strips 2" × 30½".

★ Cut 5 using 7A (template page 56).

★ Cut 8 using 4A (template page 56).

⅝ yard for binding

3¼ yards fusible web (based on 18" width)

55" × 46" for backing

assembling the quilt top

Step One

Position and pin the white stripes and blue squares to the red background before fusing them in place. This will allow you to make any adjustments, if necessary. The blue squares will overlap the ends of the white stripes by ½".

Step Two

Fuse the red circles and white stars to the blue squares.

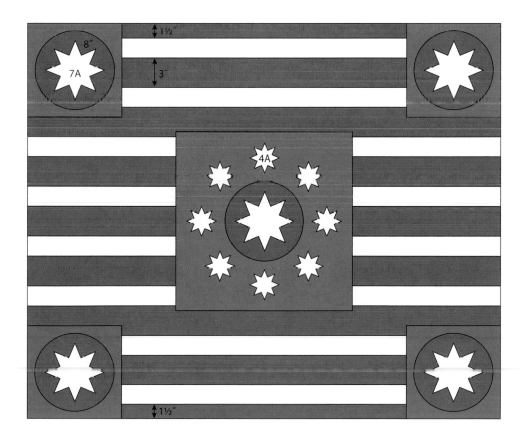

These blocks are fast and fun. For each block, I've listed the templates in the order that they should be fused to the background fabric.

basic blocks

BLOCK 1
Background: 4½″ × 4½″
Template: 3A

BLOCK 2
Background: 4½″ × 4½″
Template: 3B

BLOCK 3
Background: 5½″ × 5½″
Template: 4A

BLOCK 4
Background: 5½″ × 5½″
Template: 4B

BLOCK 5
Background: 6½″ × 6½″
Template: 5A

BLOCK 6
Background: 6½″ × 6½″
Template: 5B

basic blocks

BLOCK 7
Background: 7½″ × 7½″
Template: 6A

BLOCK 8
Background: 7½″ × 7½″
Template: 6B

BLOCK 9
Background: 8½″ × 8½″
Template: 7A

BLOCK 10
Background: 8½″ × 8½″
Template: 7B

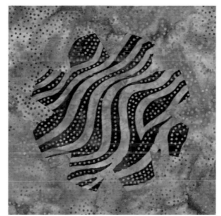

BLOCK 11
Background: 9½″ × 9½″
Template: 8A

BLOCK 12
Background: 9½″ × 9½″
Template: 8B

BLOCK 13
Background: 10½″ × 10½″
Template: 9A

BLOCK 14
Background: 10½″ × 10½″
Template: 9B

9½" blocks

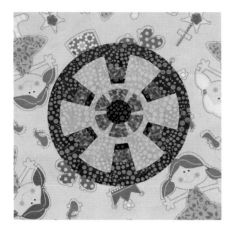

BLOCK 15

Background: 9½" × 9½"

Templates: 6" circle, 4" circle, 3" circle, 6A, 3A, 1" circle

BLOCK 16

Background: 9½" × 9½"

Templates: 7" circle, 7A cut into quarters, 2" circle, 1" circle

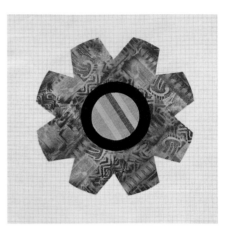

BLOCK 17

Background: 9½" × 9½"

Templates: 8A, 3" circle, 2" circle

BLOCK 18

Background: 9½" × 9½"

Templates: 7" circle (cut 7A from it; cut remaining piece into quarters), 3" circle

BLOCK 19

Background: 9½" × 9½"

Templates: 7" circle, 4A (The light circle was part of the fabric, not a template!)

BLOCK 20

Background: 9½" × 9½"

Templates: 7" circle, 6" circle, 6A, 4A

BLOCK 21

Background: 9½" × 9½"

Templates: 7" circle, 7A

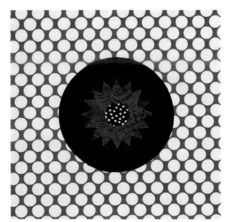

BLOCK 22

Background: 9½" × 9½"

Templates: 5" circle, two 4A, 1" circle

10½″ blocks

BLOCK 23
Background: 10½″ × 10½″
Templates: 8″ circle, 7″ circle, 6B,
four 1″ circles

BLOCK 24
Background: 10½″ × 10½″
Templates: 8″ circle, 7″ circle, 7A,
3″ circle, 4A

BLOCK 25
Background: 10½″ × 10½″
Templates: 8A, 6B, 4B, eight bonus cutouts
from 4B

BLOCK 26
Background: 10½″ × 10½″
Templates: 8″ circle, 8B, 6B, 3″ circle

BLOCK 27
Background: 10½″ × 10½″
Templates: 8″ circle, 5″ circle, 6A, three
bonus cutouts from 6A, two 1″ circles

BLOCK 28
Background: 10½″ × 10½″
Templates: 8″ circle, 8A

BLOCK 29
Background: 10½″ × 10½″
Templates: 7″ circle, 6″ circle

BLOCK 30
Background: 10½″ × 10½″
Templates: 6″ circle, 7B, one-quarter 8A for
large heart, two-quarters 5A for small hearts

BLOCK 31
Background: 10½″ × 10½″
Templates: 9A, two 5B cut into quarters,
3″ circle, 2″ circle

BLOCK 32

Background: 10½" × 10½"
Templates: 5" circle, 5A, 4A

BLOCK 33

Background: 10½" × 10½"
Templates: 7" circle cut into quarters,
6" circle, 7A, 5B

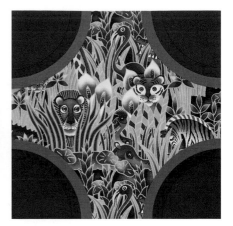

BLOCK 34

Background: 10½" × 10½"
Templates: 8" circle, 7" circle, 6" circle—
each cut into quarters

BLOCK 35

Background: 10½" × 10½"
Templates: 8B, 9B, 2" circle

BLOCK 36

Background: 10½" × 10½"
Templates: 8" circle, 8A, 4" circle, 3" circle,
2" circle

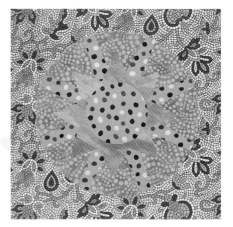

BLOCK 37

Background: 10½" × 10½"
Templates: 8" circle, 9B, 7A, 3" circle

10½" blocks

BLOCK 38
Background: 10½" × 10½"
Templates: 8" circle, 8B, 3" circle, 2" circle

BLOCK 39
Background: 10½" × 10½"
Templates: 8" circle, 9B, 4B, eight bonus
cutouts from 4B

BLOCK 40
Background: 10½" × 10½"
Templates: 9A, 7A

BLOCK 41
Background: 10½" × 10½"
Templates: 8" circle, 9B, 5B, 2" circle

BLOCK 42
Background: 10½" × 10½"
Templates: two 9B, 5A, 2" circle

BLOCK 43
Background: 10½" × 10½"
Templates: 6" circle, 9B, nine 2" circles

BLOCK 44

Background: 12½″ × 12½″

Templates: 7B cut into quarters, 8B cut into quarters, 2″ circle, 1″ circle

BLOCK 45

Background: 12½″ × 12½″

Templates: 9″ circle, 5″ circle, two 5A cut into quarters for hearts, 7A

BLOCK 46

Background: 12½″ × 12½″

Templates: 9″ circle, 9A cut into quarters

BLOCK 47

Background: 12½″ × 12½″

Templates: two 6A cut in half, 6″ circle, 5″ circle

BLOCK 48

Background: 12½″ × 12½″

Templates: 9″ circle, 8A, 3″ circle, one-quarter 8A for heart

BLOCK 49

Background: 12½″ × 12½″

Templates: 4½″ square for face; one-half 7B for beard; 7B cut in half for hair; 5B cut in half for bangs; one-quarter 3B for mouth; 2″ circle cut in half for mustache; one-half 3B cut in half for eyes; one-half 7″ circle for hat; 2″ circle for pom-pom

12½" blocks

BLOCK 50

Background: 12½" × 12½"

Templates: 9" circle, 6" circle (cut 6A from it; cut remaining piece into six pieces), 3" circle

BLOCK 51

Background: 12½" × 12½"

Templates: 5" circle, 9B, 3" circle, eight 1" circles, eight bonus cutouts from 9B

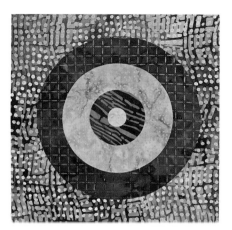

BLOCK 52

Background: 12½" × 12½"

Templates: 9" circle, 6" circle, 3" circle, 1" circle

BLOCK 53

Background: 12½" × 12½"

Templates: 9B cut into quarters, 9A, 6" circle

BLOCK 54

Background: 12½" × 12½"

Templates: 9" circle, 7A, 3" circle, two 4B, 4A, 2" circle

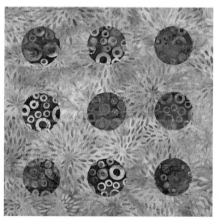

BLOCK 55

Background: 12½" × 12½"

Templates: nine 2" circles

BLOCK 56

Background: 12½" × 12½"

Templates: four 5B cut in half, 8A cut into quarters, 5A cut into quarters

BLOCK 57

Background: 12½" × 12½"

Templates: 9B, 8A, 7B, 3" circle, 2" circle, three bonus cutouts from 8A

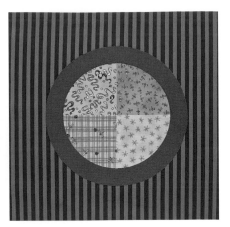

BLOCK 58

Background: 12½" × 12½"

Templates: 8" circle, 6" circle cut from four 3½" squares sewn together

BLOCK 59

Background: 12½" × 12½"

Templates: 9A, 8B, 3" circle

BLOCK 60

Background: 12½" × 12½"

Templates: 9" circle, 9B, 3" circle, eight 1" circles

BLOCK 61

Background: 12½" × 12½"

Templates: 9" circle, 8A, 5A, 2" circle

12½″ blocks

BLOCK 62
Background: 12½″ × 12½″
Templates: 8″ circle, 6″ circle cut into quarters, four 3A

BLOCK 63
Background: 12½″ × 12½″
Templates: 9A, two 5B cut into quarters, 3″ circle, 2″ circle

BLOCK 64
Background: 12½″ × 12½″
Templates: 4″ circle, two 6B cut in half, one 6B cut into quarters

BLOCK 65
Background: 12½″ × 12½″
Templates: 7″ circle, 6B cut into quarters, 2″ circle, 1″ circle, two 5B cut into quarters

BLOCK 66
Background: 12½″ × 12½″
Templates: 7B, 7A, 5A

BLOCK 67
Background: 12½″ × 12½″
Templates: 9″ circle, 5″ circle, 7A, 2″ circle

12½″ blocks

BLOCK 68
Background: 12½″ × 12½″
Templates: 9″ circle, 9A, 7B, 2″ circle

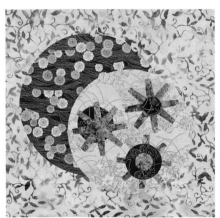

BLOCK 69
Background: 12½″ × 12½″
Templates: 8″ circle, 7″ circle, two 2″ circles, two 1″ circles, three 4B

BLOCK 70
Background: 12½″ × 12½″
Templates: 9″ circle, 8A, 7A, 4B

BLOCK 71
Background: 12½″ × 12½″
Templates: 9″ circle, 9B, four 3B, four 1″ circles, 5B, 2″ circle

BLOCK 72
Background: 12½″ × 12½″
Templates: 9A, 8B, 6B, 3B, 1″ circle

BLOCK 73
Background: 12½″ × 12½″
Templates: 9″ circle, 9B, eight bonus cutouts from 9B, 5A, 4A

12½" blocks

BLOCK 74
Background: 12½" × 12½"
Templates: 8" circle, 7B, 9B, 7A, 5B

BLOCK 75
Background: 12½" × 12½"
Templates: 8B, 9B, 4A

BLOCK 76
Background: 12½" × 12½"
Templates: 9" circle, six 4A

BLOCK 77
Background: 12½" × 12½"
Templates: 6" circle for face; 5B and two 3B cut in half for collars; 4A cut in half for hair; one-half 8A for hat; 4B for flower; 2" circle for nose; two-quarters (one-half) 3B for big part of eyes; 1" circle cut into quarters for small part of eyes and sides of mouth

BLOCK 78
Background: 12½" × 12½"
Templates: 8" circle, 8A, 4" circle, 4B, eight bonus cutouts from 4B

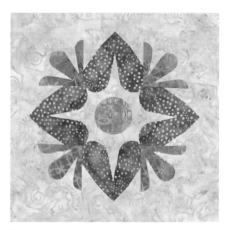

BLOCK 79
Background: 12½" × 12½"
Templates: 2" circle, 8B cut into quarters, 6B cut into quarters

12½" blocks

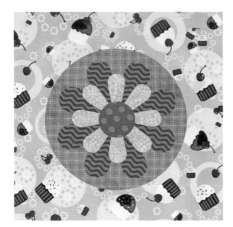

BLOCK 80
Background: 12½" × 12½"
Templates: 8" circle, 8B, 6B, 2" circle

BLOCK 81
Background: 12½" × 12½"
Templates: 9" circle, 7A cut in half, 4A cut in half, 5" circle, 2" circle, two 4A

BLOCK 82
Background: 12½" × 12½"; sew two 6½" × 12½" rectangles together
Templates: 8" circle cut from two 4½" × 8½" rectangles sewn together

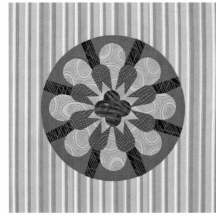

BLOCK 83
Background: 12½" × 12½"
Templates: 8" circle, 9B, 8B, 6B, 4A, 3B

BLOCK 84
Background: 12½" × 12½"
Templates: 9" circle, 6" circle cut into quarters, 5" circle

14½" blocks

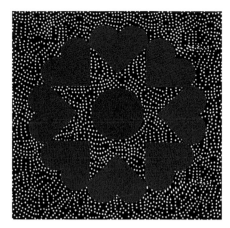

BLOCK 85
Background: 14½" × 14½"
Templates: two 9A cut into quarters, 3" circle

BLOCK 86
Background: 14½" × 14½"
Templates: two 9B cut in half, 5" circle

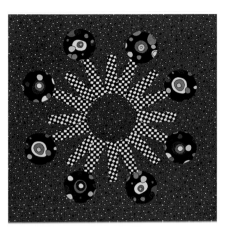

BLOCK 87
Background: 14½" × 14½"
Templates: two 9B, 3" circle, eight 2" circles

BLOCK 88
Background: 14½" × 14½"
Templates: 5" circle, 4" circle, and 3" circle for snowman; 2" circle and 3A for snowballs; 2" × 3" rectangle for hat (trim corners); ½" × 3½" rectangle for brim of hat; 1" circle for pom-pom; freehand cut arms and stars

BLOCK 89
Background: 14½" × 14½"
Templates: two 9A cut into quarters, 6B, 1" circle

BLOCK 90
Background: 14½" × 14½"; sew four 7½" squares together
Template: 9" circle

14½" blocks

BLOCK 91

Background: 14½" × 14½"

Templates: two 9B cut in half, 6" circle, 7A, 2" circle

BLOCK 92

Background: 14½" × 14½"

Templates: 5A, 2" circle, two 8B cut in half

BLOCK 93

Background: 14½" × 14½"

Templates: four 5" circles, 8A cut into quarters

15½" blocks

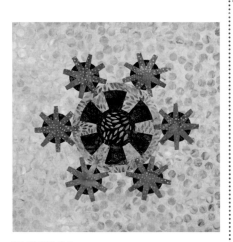

BLOCK 94

Background: 14½" × 14½"

Templates: 6" circle, 6A, seven 3" circles, six 4B

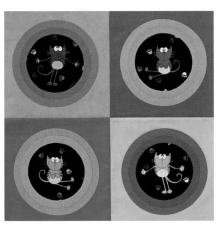

BLOCK 95

Background: 15½" × 15½"; sew four 8" squares together

Templates: four 6" circles, four 5" circles, four 4" circles

BLOCK 96

Background: 15½" × 15½"

Templates: 9B, 3A, eight 4B

18½" blocks

BLOCK 97
Background: 18½" × 18½"
Templates: 8" circle, 7A, eight 4A

BLOCK 98
Background: 18½" × 18½"
Templates: four 7" circles, four 6A, four 1" circles, 7A

rectangular blocks

BLOCK 99
Background: 14½" × 16½"
Templates: one-half 8A for base of basket,
8" circle; use 9B to cut out top part for
stems; two 3" circles, two 3A, and two
1" circles for smaller flowers; 4" circle,
5B, 4B, and 1" circle for large flower

BLOCK 100
Background: 10½" × 19½"
Templates: 9B cut into quarters
for tree. use three quarters for
branches, then cut remaining
quarter in half, and use one piece
for lower trunk and one bonus
cutout for base of tree; three 5B
cut into quarters for ornaments
(use nine); 4A for star

String Art by Janet McCarroll

SIZE: 42″ × 42″

BLOCKS: 31, 44, 52, 61, 63, 67, 72, 80, 84

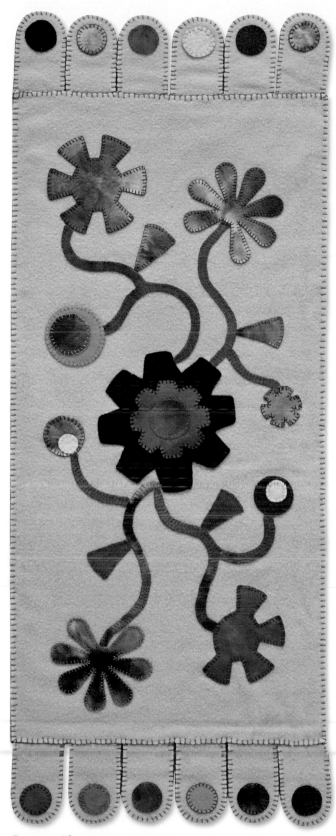

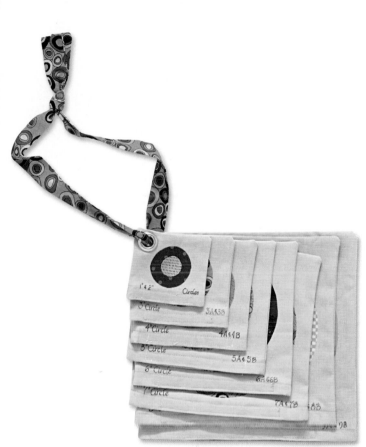

Tote for templates by Beth Anne Lowrie

TEMPLATES: All. Each pocket is 1½″ larger than the template, with a Velcro opening along the bottom. The grommets are ⅞₆″, made by Dritz. For quick and easy reference, fuse a sample of the templates to each pocket and use a permanent marker for labeling.

Cottage Blossoms by Ellen Pahl

SIZE: 15½″ × 40″

TEMPLATES: 8A, 6A, 6B, 5A, 3A, 3″ circle, 2″ circle, 1″ circle

Button-Flower Pockets by Liz Aneloski

SIZE: 25½" × 25½"

TEMPLATES: 9" circle, 6" circle, 3" circle, 6A, 3A

Happy Times by Laura Reidenbach

SIZE: 35" × 35"

TEMPLATES: *Sun:* 7A, 4A, 1" circle;
Clown: 3" circle, 1" circle, 7A, 4A, 4B, 3B;
Flower: 7B, 6B, 3A, 1" circle;
Balloons: 4" circle, 3" circle, 2" circle,
3A (some were modified)

Dream Garden by Pam Quentin,
quilted by Linda Engelbrecht

SIZE: 53″ × 58″

TEMPLATES: All (some were modified).
Leaves, stems, and vines
were made by cutting the 9″ circle
into different shapes.

Avenue T by Pam Quentin,
quilted by Linda Engelbrecht

SIZE: 65″ × 74″

TEMPLATES: All templates were
used for trees and flowers
(some were modified). House
and tree patterns can be found in
Nancy's *Big Block Quilts by Magic*
(by C&T Publishing).

Color Wheel by Nancy Jones,
quilted by Linda Engelbrecht

SIZE: 59½″ × 60″

TEMPLATES: 7A, 6B, 5B, 4A, 4B, 3A, 3B,
2″ circle, 1″ circle

Transitions by Nancy Jones,
quilted by Linda Engelbrecht

SIZE: 51″ × 46½″

TEMPLATES: 8″ circle, 2″ circle,
1″ circle, 8A, 8B, 7A, 7B, 6A,
6B, 5A, 5B, 4A, 4B

Pillows by Debbie Donowski

SIZE: 16″ × 16″

TEMPLATES: 9″ circle, 7″ circle, 6″ circle, 2″ circle, 1″ circle, 8B, 6B (some were modified)

Gears by Debbie Donowski

SIZE: 31″ × 33″

TEMPLATES: 2″ circle, 1″ circle, 9B, 8A, 6A, 5A, 4B, 3A (some were modified)

The Tree of Dreams mandala by Allison Dowling

SIZE: 30″ × 30″

TEMPLATES: 6″ circle, 3″ circle, 2″ circle, 1″ circle, 8B,
7A, 5A, 5B, 4A, 4B, 3A, 3B (some were modified)

Kaleidoscope Dream by Robin Fleming

SIZE: 31″ × 31″

TEMPLATES: 9″ circle, 5″ circle, 8A, 5B (some were modified)

The Big "J" by Janet McCarroll

SIZE: 39″ × 61½″

TEMPLATES: All

Sunny beach bag by Janet McCarroll

SIZE: 19½″ × 22″

TEMPLATES: 3″ circle, 9A, 7A, 7B

Little girl's sundress by Beth Anne Lowrie

TEMPLATES: 1" circle, 8A, 3B (some were modified)

Mother–daughter beach cover-ups by Beth Anne Lowrie

TEMPLATES: 6" circle, 2" circle, 8B, 6A, 6B, 4B, 3B (some were modified)

scrapbook and blank board book gallery

The templates in this book (pages 56–62) also work very well with Blank Board Books (by C&T Publishing) and scrapbooking supplies.

"Love Is a Circle without an End" scrapbook by Debbie Donowski

"Halloween" scrapbook by Debbie Donowski

"Senior Year" scrapbook by Debbie Donowski

"Our Universe" scrapbook by Allison Dowling

Family scrapbook by Jenny and Casey Srebro

"Families Are Like Fudge" scrapbook by Rocky Sidorek

Scrapbook by Carol Brown

Purse scrapbook by Vicki Novajosky

Scrapbook by Allison Dowling

House scrapbook by Jenny and Casey Srebro

template patterns

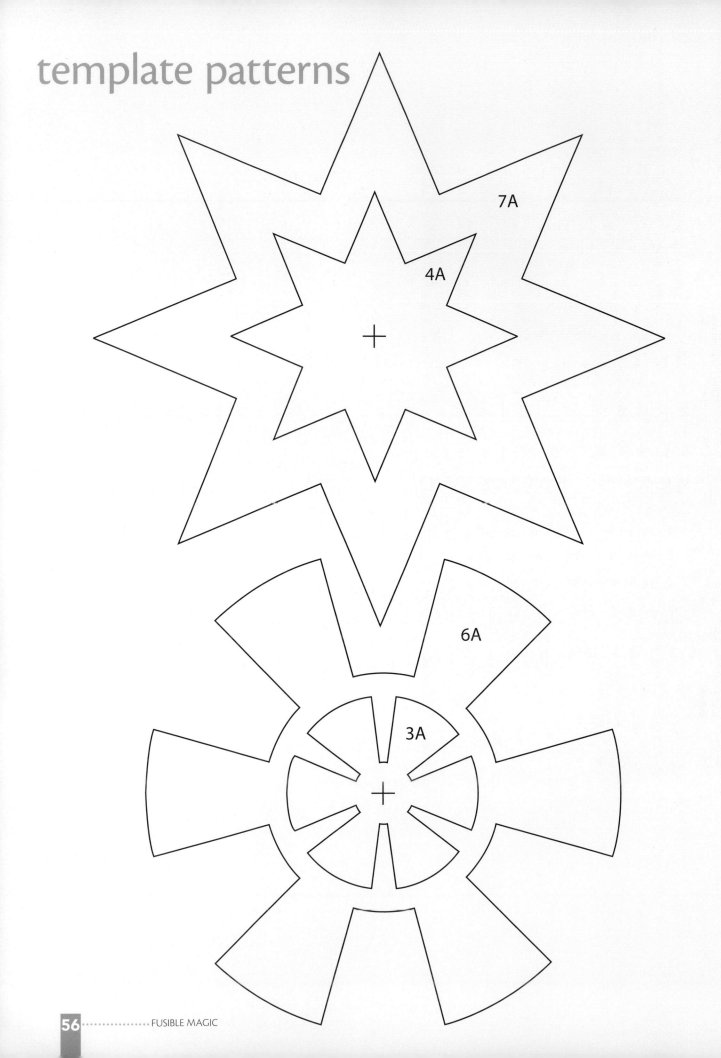

7A

4A

6A

3A

8B

6B

5B

3B

Leaf for Gathering Basket

8A

5A

Leaf for Happy Go Lucky

Leaf for Happy Go Lucky

9B

4B

Leaf for Floral Salute

9A

7B

7B

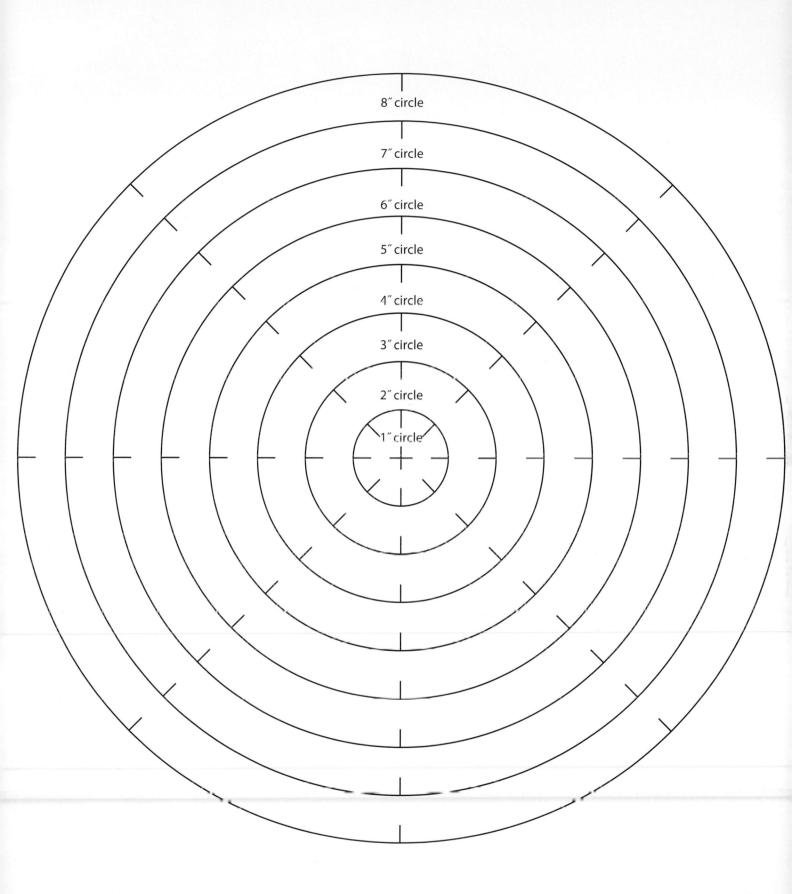

8″ circle

7″ circle

6″ circle

5″ circle

4″ circle

3″ circle

2″ circle

1″ circle

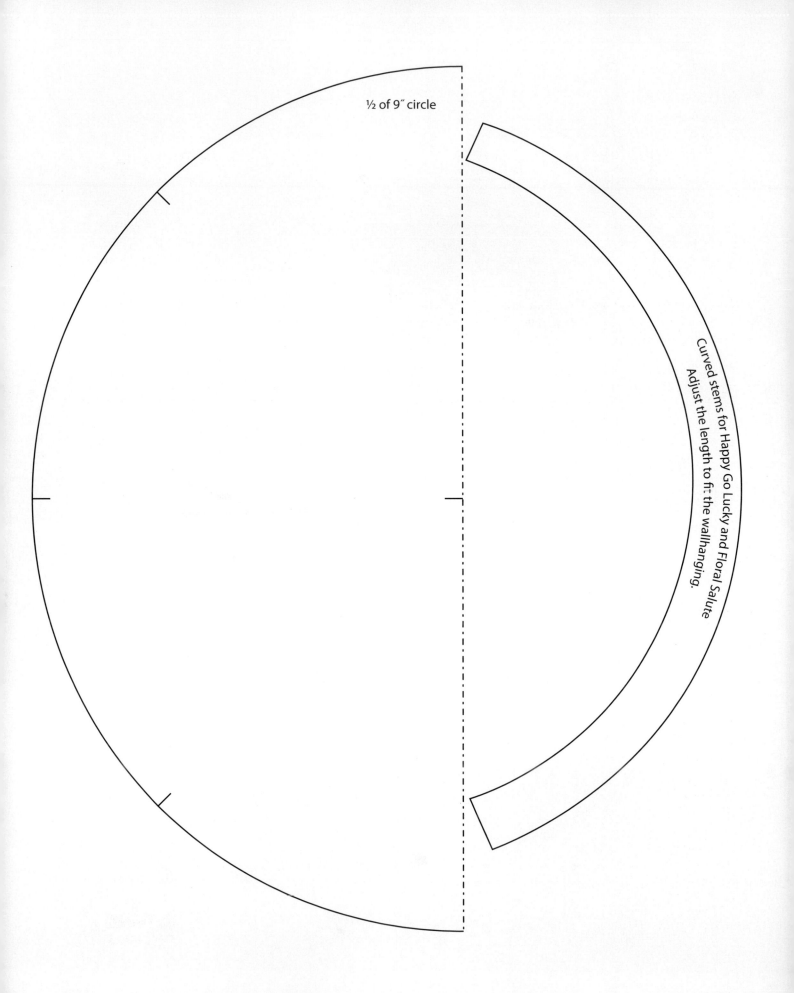

½ of 9″ circle

Curved stems for Happy Go Lucky and Floral Salute
Adjust the length to fit the wallhanging.

resources

- **American & Efird, Inc.**
  www.amefird.com
  Exclusive importers of Mettler threads to the USA

- **Bernina of America, Inc.**
  www.berninausa.com
  Bernina sewing machines

- **Creative Impressions**
  www.creativeimpressions.com
  Scrapbooking products

- **Fairfield Processing Corp.**
  www.poly-fil.com
  Batting, pillow inserts

- **FreeSpirit**
  www.freespiritfabric.com
  Fabric

- **Grafix**
  www.grafixarts.com
  Scrapbooking products

- **Hambly Screen Prints**
  www.HamblyScreenPrints.com
  Scrapbooking products

- **Marcus Fabrics**
  www.MarcusFabrics.com
  Fabric

- **P&B Textiles**
  www.pbtex.com
  Fabric

- **Prym Consumer USA Inc.**
  www.dritz.com
  www.omnigrid.com
  Omnigrid rulers, scissors, clear plastic template material, appliqué pressing cloth, 28mm & 45mm rotary cutters, Flip-N-Cut Magic Templates by Omnigrid, Invisi-Grip

- **Robert Kaufman Co, Inc.**
  www.robertkaufman.com
  Fabric

- **Timeless Treasures**
  www.ttfabrics.com
  Fabric

- **The Warm Company**
  www.warmcompany.com
  Batting, Steam-A-Steam 2 fusible web

- **Westminster Fibers – Lifestyle Fabrics**
  www.westminsterfabrics.com
  Fabric

about the author

Grandma Garrison was Nancy's mentor while she made her first quilt in 1972. Gram asked her to cut a six-inch square template from paper and pin it on some fabric. Using regular scissors, quite dull, Nancy cut around the paper template. After cutting about two dozen squares, she noticed that some of the squares were not the same size. Nancy called Gram and said, "My blocks don't seem to be the same size." Gram replied, "Are you cutting any of the paper template off when you cut around it?" Nancy replied, "No, only once in a while!" That was Nancy's first lesson in accuracy, and it has stuck with her all these years. Today her hallmark is accuracy, and she stresses it with students and attributes the wide recognition of her work to its continued emphasis.

She has written several best-selling books, including *Featherweight 221: The Perfect Portable* and *Rotary Magic*. Nancy also refined how to work with squares and rectangles in her other best-selling books *Block Magic*, *Stars by Magic*, and *Big One-Star Quilts by Magic*. Recently she was granted a U.S. patent for her innovative technique used for making eight-point stars from squares and rectangles.

Nancy has been a spokesperson and consultant for Omnigrid, a division of Prym Consumer USA Inc., for more than twenty years.

Her hobbies include reading mysteries, traveling to see children and grandchildren, working in her flower gardens (they keep expanding), and making quilts for charity. In recent years she has donated more than a thousand quilts to brighten the lives of needy children and veterans. Nancy lives in Pennsylvania with her husband, Frank.

Also by Nancy Johnson-Srebro

Great Titles *from* C&T PUBLISHING

Available at your local retailer or **www.ctpub.com** *or* **800-284-1114**